ACKNOWLEDGEMENTS

We would like to thank Amy Merone, Will Sutcliffe, Penny Walker, Kathryn Cousins, Dr Omer El-Hamdoon, Gina Clayton, Gill Buttery, Dr Vithal Patel and Donna Jones for their contributions to this handbook. We are also grateful to the people who agreed to be interviewed for our case studies, and to all those who are working to make their communities places of safety and welcome for people seeking sanctuary.

Thanks also to Leicester Faiths Support Group for Asylum Seekers and refugees for permission to reproduce extracts from their booklet 'Scriptures and Traditions and the care of Asylum Seekers and Refugees' (2008).

Finally, we are grateful to Sheffield Faiths Forum and the Yorkshire & Humber Faiths Forum for their financial support for this publication.

First published in 2009 by Plug and Tap,
16 Sycamore Business Park, Copt Hewick, Ripon HG4 5DF
www.plugandtap.co.uk

A catalogue record for this book is available from the
British Library

ISBN 978-0-9562120-0-9

CONTENTS

INTRODUCTION

Around July 2005 I began to wonder, could Sheffield become a recognised *'City of Sanctuary'* for asylum seekers and refugees? I shared the idea with Craig Barnett. Together we began to work on the idea.

Many people are now familiar with the idea of a 'Fairtrade City', in which a wide range of community groups and organisations make a commitment to using and selling fair-trade goods. In a similar way, a *'City of Sanctuary'*, we imagined, would be a place where schools, community groups, faith groups and cultural organisations, as well as local government, were committed to offering hospitality and support to refugees and asylum-seekers in their communities.

Many people who support refugees and asylum-seekers - those seeking sanctuary - experience the difficulty of constantly reacting to ever-harsher legislation and media coverage. It can be difficult to feel a sense of achievement or progress towards a more hospitable and humane society. Working towards *'City of Sanctuary'* status for Sheffield we felt it would represent a positive common goal and aspiration for a wide variety of organisations, groups and individuals. Just as with a 'Fairtrade City', it could embody a set of explicit goals for the number of local organisations that signed up to the initiative, and a commitment to broaden support for the idea in order to gradually influence the culture of the city as a whole.

Sheffield has an excellent record of support for asylum-seekers and refugees, and a diverse and thriving multicultural population. This made it ideally placed to be the first city to adopt the goal of becoming a *'City of Sanctuary'* for people in need of safety from persecution.

Following a meeting on 15th October 2005, to discuss Sanctuary, many organisations adopted the following resolution:

"Our organisation recognises the contribution of asylum-seekers and refugees to the City of Sheffield, and is committed to welcoming and including them in our activities. We support Sheffield being a recognised *'City of Sanctuary'* for refugees and asylum-seekers."

Almost 100 organisations have signed up so far, including community organisations, worship centres, Students Unions of both our Universities, a number of businesses, our faith leaders from different faiths, and our City Council that represents different political persuasions. In September 2007 Sheffield became the UK's first City of Sanctuary.

On 4th June 2008, over 100 people from 23 different towns and cities in England, Wales and Scotland met to hear the story of developments in Sheffield. They went back to their own contexts to explore how their own area could follow Sheffield's lead.

There are now City of Sanctuary working groups in Bradford, Bristol, Coventry, Hull, Nottingham, Swansea, Leicester, Oxford and London. The Refugee Council and Refugee Action are supporting the City of Sanctuary movement nationally.

The City of Sanctuary movement creates an opportunity to work with local people to counter some of the hostile attitudes that drive government policy and to create a culture of hospitality and welcome. The Sanctuary's work has been recognised regionally and expected to become part of the regional approach to cohesion.

This work is urgent and important in our times of open hostility and hatred towards people who come here seeking protection and security – fleeing the torture of persecution or poverty.

The significant fact about City of Sanctuary is that it is a grassroots movement. The lesson from Sheffield is to involve people and organisations from all backgrounds, to create a groundswell of support and an unstoppable momentum.

This book offers some practical lessons and insights from the Sanctuary movement that has emerged, and also some inspirational stories to draw on.

Go for it!

Inderjit Bhogal
Chair, City of Sanctuary
April 2009

ONE

'Proud to be a Place of Safety' – The Vision and History of the City of Sanctuary Movement

A City of Sanctuary is a place of safety and welcome for people whose lives are in danger in their own countries.

It is a place where:

- the skills and cultures of people seeking sanctuary are valued, where they are included in local communities and able to contribute to the life of the city.

- community groups, local government, media, business, schools and colleges have a shared commitment to offering sanctuary, so that it is seen as part of the city's identity by local people.

- people seeking sanctuary can easily build relationships with local people as neighbours, friends and colleagues. Through these relationships, local people come to understand the injustices refugees face, and become motivated to support and defend them.

This vision is obviously an ultimate goal rather than a current reality. There is nowhere that this vision has been fully achieved, although in many towns and cities across Britain there are already elements of it in practice, and some of them are described in this book.

Is there any value in such an idealistic and perhaps unachievable goal? It is important to have a positive vision, which can motivate people to work together towards its realisation. A vision can give us a sense of direction and common purpose, which is especially important for people who have experienced the continual demoralisation of a decade of increasingly punitive asylum policy.

Of course the reality in much of the UK is a widespread, largely unthinking public hostility towards refugees and 'asylum-seekers', largely created by decades of sustained media scapegoating. According to research by the Independent Asylum Commission ('Saving Sanctuary', p 15) the British general public have learned to associate the term 'asylum-seeker' with illegal immigrants, benefit cheats and criminality, but do not recognise it as referring to people seeking safety from persecution.

Government policy over the last few decades has also been driven by these public attitudes. Through a series of increasingly harsh changes to the asylum system our society has created a separate class of people, who can be arrested in dawn raids and detained indefinitely without charge or trial (including children), made destitute without the right to work or benefits, and forcibly deported to repressive regimes, in some cases resulting in their death (Independent 17th March 09). No town or city in the UK can be completely safe for people in need of sanctuary until this system is radically changed.

At the same time there are many people of goodwill whose voices are rarely heard. These include people who have come into contact with refugees as their neighbours, students, and friends, and have been scandalised by the injustices they experience.

This is not exclusively a middle-class experience. In fact it is the local people who live in the housing estates and inner-city areas who are most likely to have day to day contact with people seeking sanctuary as neighbours, parents and classmates. Although these contacts can be a source of friction, they can also lead to relationships of mutual support and friendship. One single mother from Syria, who lives in a housing estate in a deprived area of Sheffield, has become friends with several of her British neighbours. She has shared babysitting with her neighbours, and even looked after one of her daughter's British friends for several days to help their family at a time of illness.

This is a common, but often unnoticed situation in towns and cities throughout Britain. Paradoxically, the 'dispersal system' which has forced people seeking sanctuary to live in areas of the country with little previous experience of refugees, has also created new communities of support for them all over the UK.

Working towards becoming a City of Sanctuary is a way of mobilising this support, and giving a voice to people of goodwill who are usually unheard in a public debate that is dominated by the loud and aggressive voices of hostility towards refugees. A City of Sanctuary initiative aims to build this potential support into a city-wide movement that can influence the culture of the communities where people seeking sanctuary live, and the practice of local organisations and government.

City of Sanctuary aims to emphasise the positive values of hospitality and friendship with people seeking sanctuary. We want to promote a discussion that emphasises a community's sense of pride in the way it responds to new arrivals. This approach goes beyond representing people seeking sanctuary as simply victims. Instead we encourage and celebrate mutual relationships of support, learning and friendship between local people and new arrivals.

For people who have sought sanctuary to feel genuinely welcome in their community, fully accepted and able to contribute, there needs to be a culture of hospitality. A culture can't be imposed or engineered by governments; it is the responsibility of everyone. A culture is built by the conversations people have in the shops, at the school gate and on the bus; by the ways they interact with each other, their interest in each other and their willingness to build relationships and make connections. Everyone can contribute to building a culture of hospitality in the places where they live and work.

A city which knows how to welcome people seeking sanctuary is a better place for everyone. The focus of City of Sanctuary is on people who have been forced to leave their home countries to seek sanctuary in the UK, but a place with a culture of hospitality will be more welcoming not just for people in need of sanctuary, but for anyone who is newly arrived for whatever reason, or who might be isolated or vulnerable. It will be a better place for local people too. It means that a city will not become a stagnant, fearful inward-looking place, but will benefit from a flow of new ideas, talents and relationships.

The ultimate aim of the national City of Sanctuary movement is to build a network of towns and cities throughout the UK, which are demonstrating their commitment to being places of safety for people in need of sanctuary. This is one of our best opportunities to create 'political space' for change at a national level, by demonstrating the desire of people of goodwill for a more just and humane approach to offering sanctuary to refugees.

Cities are powerful. They can't be ignored as lobby groups or single-issue campaigners. A nationwide network of towns and cities that are committed to welcoming people in need of sanctuary has a huge potential to influence political debate and government policy.

Our society faces critical challenges in the coming years, with the prospect of continued economic crisis, unemployment, and escalating climate change and energy shortages. All of these have the tendency to create growing xenophobia, distrust and resentment of refugees. Without a sustained and effective movement to rebuild the UK's commitment to offering sanctuary, we could find ourselves in a society of ever harsher border controls, growing government repression and public hostility.

The tradition of providing sanctuary for people whose lives are in danger is precious. It has its roots in the oldest human cultures. It is recognised by every faith and in international law through the 1951 UN Charter on Refugees, and it has saved countless lives. It is a deeply British tradition and is crucial to preserving a good society. But it needs to be practised, not allowed to degenerate into tabloid scapegoating and resentment that leads to a fortress Britain, with detention centres and dawn arrests of schoolchildren. It needs champions who are prepared to speak up for sanctuary as something to be proud of, something that can unite different communities around a positive vision for their city.

Reviving the tradition of sanctuary is something the world is going to need very much in the coming decades. The City of Sanctuary movement is one way that each of us in the UK can contribute to that revival, and help to hand it on to future generations in a better condition than we have found it.

History of the City of Sanctuary movement

The City of Sanctuary movement began as the idea of Inderjit Bhogal, a former President of the UK Methodist Conference who has campaigned for many years on behalf of refugees and other excluded people.

It was inspired partly by the success of the Fairtrade Towns movement in bringing issues of trade justice into the mainstream of British society, but also by the existence of passionate and broad-based local support for people seeking sanctuary in Sheffield. The concept also has roots in Jewish and Christian scripture and history, and powerful links with other faith traditions, which are explored in the following chapter.

In October 2005 some of those who were most involved in supporting and befriending refugees in Sheffield met to explore the idea of a City of Sanctuary. At that meeting, we decided to go out to the various community organisations we had contact with, and ask for formal resolutions of support for the goal of becoming the UK's first City of Sanctuary.

A small committee of volunteers was set up to oversee the initiative, with a simple constitution and some small grants from local individuals and faith groups. Craig Barnett also began as a volunteer working two days a week, acting as co-ordinator for our supporters' network, and later received financial support from Sheffield Quakers to continue this work.

Over the following months, City of Sanctuary volunteers organised a variety of public events to publicise the initiative. These included speakers' events where refugees spoke about their experience of life in Sheffield, Ceilidh dances, concerts and parties at which local people and refugees could meet and socialise together.

In this way a mailing list was built up of several hundred supporters across the city who became advocates for the City of Sanctuary initiative in their faith groups, community centres, Community Forums, student groups and social clubs. We were invited to speak to many local groups, and also encouraged them to invite refugee speakers from an awareness-raising project which trained and supported volunteers to do this work.

Through an email newsletter to our supporters we were able to publicise opportunities for contact with refugee communities, including volunteer placements, language exchanges, and social events. We were also able to advertise the needs of refugee groups for volunteers, emergency accommodation, furniture etc to a growing network, as supporting organisations passed on information to their memberships, many of whom had little previous contact with people seeking sanctuary.

We also produced and distributed free postcards of Sheffield Peace Gardens designed by local artist Pete McKee, which represented our vision of Sheffield as a City of Sanctuary. Volunteers distributed City of Sanctuary beermats around Sheffield's pubs and cafes, as a way of creating talking points among people who were not necessarily natural supporters.

With a small grant from Sheffield City Council, we also printed signs reading 'We welcome asylum-seekers & refugees', which supporting organisations could display outside their buildings. Gradually, these started to appear outside about 60 churches, student unions and offices around the city as a visible sign of growing support for the movement.

Thanks to our volunteer Mark Gibbens, who is a professional Web-designer (www.seedlingmedia.co.uk), we soon had our own website, featuring news of our events, and we encouraged supporting organisations to provide links to this from their own websites.

The Mayor of Sheffield during 2006, Cllr Jackie Drayton, was another advocate for the new movement. She displayed our 'welcome' sign prominently on her desk and discussed it with her visitors, and this helped to raise awareness of the movement within the Town Hall and beyond.

When we held our initial 'Towards a City of Sanctuary' meeting in October 2005, we speculated that if the initiative was successful in building grassroots support, in four or five years we might even be able to persuade the City Council to sign up to it.

In fact, in early 2007 we were informed that Sheffield City Council had cross-party support for becoming a City of Sanctuary. The new Mayor made a formal announcement of the Council's support at the launch of Refugee Week in June 2007.

With around 70 supporting organisations throughout the city and the Council's official endorsement, we decided to hold an official media launch of Sheffield as the UK's first City of Sanctuary in September 2007. The Mayor held a reception for representatives of some of our supporting organisations at the Town Hall, and the story was picked up by BBC Radio 4 and 5, and The Guardian, as well as local radio and newspapers.

As news of our launch spread, people from other cities began contacting us to ask how they could become Cities of Sanctuary too. We received funding from the Joseph Rowntree Charitable Trust to develop a national support network for other City of Sanctuary groups, and held our first national conference in June 2008, with around a hundred participants from 23 towns and cities. National charities The Refugee Council and Refugee Action also decided to offer their support to help the national movement to develop.

By April 2009 there were ten established City of Sanctuary groups in major cities from Bradford to London, with several more at the planning stage. Representatives of the local groups meet regularly to share learning and experiences, and to make decisions affecting the whole movement. We have developed a more formal set of criteria and a process for becoming a recognised City of Sanctuary, which is discussed in Chapter 6. We also have a growing set of shared resources, a national website and lots of collaborative working developing. This includes a national tour of the play 'Asylum Dialogues' for Refugee Week 2009, and plans for a Parliamentary Adjournment Debate on the City of Sanctuary movement with the support of MPs from 'our' cities.

Many of the local City of Sanctuary groups have already built impressive movements of supporters, and some are well on their way to meeting the full City of Sanctuary criteria. Local groups have also been finding creative ways to interpret the City of Sanctuary vision for their own local history and context. In Leicester, this includes the experience of Ugandan Asians who moved there in the 1970s, and have been an important influence on the local economy and culture. In Bristol, City of Sanctuary has been welcomed as a way of making reparations for the city's role in the transatlantic slave trade.

In Sheffield, it has been heartening to hear refugees and local people taking pride in Sheffield's status as a City of Sanctuary, and using it to celebrate their achievements and also to hold local government accountable. We are also working with Sheffield City Council to translate their commitment to being a City of Sanctuary into practice. We have developed a City of Sanctuary Manifesto, with contributions from all of our supporters, which became official Council policy in February 2009. We also continue to work at broadening support for people seeking sanctuary throughout Sheffield's communities, in the arts, the media, in business and education. We recognise that becoming an 'official' City of Sanctuary doesn't mean that we are now the place of safety and welcome that we are working for. We still have much to do, and no city can be a place of complete safety until we have built enough public support throughout the country for a new approach to the asylum system which protects the safety and dignity of everyone in the UK.

City of Sanctuary groups as at April 09

Sheffield
Leicester
Bradford
Nottingham
Coventry
Oxford
London
Bristol
Swansea
Hull

Sheffield Live! 93.2 FM

The volunteers at Sheffield Live! make the community radio station what it is. Each week shows go out in community languages, and presenters make the effort to go out and speak to people in different parts of the city. The station also offers free training on

Photo: Mildred & Claire at Sheffield Live!

radio journalism skills, making a particular effort to engage with young people in no formal education. Alan, the station's programme co-ordinator, felt it was natural that people seeking sanctuary were involved at Sheffield Live! as two of the key aims of the station are to represent the city's diversity and to be open to all.

The station shows its commitment to welcoming people seeking sanctuary in Sheffield in many ways. One example is its regular coverage of issues related to asylum seekers and refugees in the city. Sheffield Live! also presents special features for World Refugee Day each year. As part of its aim to represent those voices which aren't often heard in the mainstream media, it also offers people seeking sanctuary the chance to take part in the training courses. After completing the training they have the opportunity to present their own radio show.

Claire and Mildred have both been involved in the station for about two years. They are not allowed to get paid work, as they are still waiting for their refugee status, yet at Sheffield Live! they have been able to get involved in a project which is fun, creative and where they can develop useful skills.

Claire explained the difference being involved in the show has made to her language skills: "When I started here my English wasn't good, and it has improved so much thanks to the show." Claire and Mildred started off not knowing a thing about radio journalism, and now both are able to train new people themselves.

Another keen volunteer is Ouattara, originally from the Ivory Coast, now seeking sanctuary in Sheffield. Ouattara completed training up to Level 3 Radio Journalism at Sheffield Live! and he is now one of the station's senior duty managers. During the shows Ouattara took part in, he particularly enjoyed going out to interview people, and even got the opportunity to interview the world famous football player Pele. The volunteering he does now gives him experience in a position of responsibility, which would be a great inclusion on his CV one day.

Alan explained that the key thing in all their work is to treat people equally and with respect: "Sheffield Live! welcomes anyone in Sheffield. Internally, we don't identify certain people as being asylum seekers and others not."

The advice Alan gives to other organisations is to understand what their own values are first. "Ask yourself whether this is the kind of thing that you would want to support. If your values are such that you want to welcome asylum seekers and refugees, and you want to involve those people in the station, then make sure that they know about those opportunities."

Alan emphasises the importance of treating people equally: "From my point of view, refugees and asylum seekers want to be treated the same way as anyone else. If they know that it is an open opportunity that anyone can apply for, then that makes them feel more respected. The main thing is we want people to know that they are welcome, regardless of their Home Office status."

Danewood/Pipworth Youth Group, Sheffield

In 2007, as part of the UNHCR Gateway Protection Programme, a group of families from Burma's Karen ethnic minority family were offered sanctuary in Sheffield. One of the families was moved onto the Lower Manor Estate, an area with many social problems and a poor reputation in the city for anti-social behaviour. They were the only Karen family on the Manor, could speak no English and were initially very isolated.

A group of young people based at the Woodthorpe youth centre met the family's two boys, aged 11 and 13, and decided to invite them to join their youth group. Young people from the group have donated toys and a bicycle to the younger children, challenged racist behaviour towards them, and even learnt some of the Karen language. In September 2008, the youth group organised a local street party and community barbecue, inviting local residents and the Karen community from across the city to meet each other. Some of the Karen families who took part said that this was the first event they had been invited to by local people.

To mark the first anniversary of Sheffield as a City of Sanctuary, the Danewood/Pipworth youth group were chosen for a City of Sanctuary award, for their contribution to making Sheffield a place of safety and welcome. This was presented to them by the Mayor of Sheffield at the Town Hall (pictured – notice the cheeky one with his tongue out...), and received positive coverage from local press.

Greenfingers, Sheffield

Photo: a gardener at the Greenfingers project

Greenfingers is a gardening project for adults with mental health problems living in the Burngreave area of Sheffield. They offer the opportunity to work on the allotment for two days a week, with volunteer support workers. Yet what they're offering isn't just about gardening – the project provides many other benefits, such as outdoor activity and exercise, time and space to unwind, an opportunity to meet people and make new friends, or just get some distraction from what's troubling them.

A few years ago, the Asylum Seeker Health Team referred one of their clients to the project. Since then Greenfingers have welcomed around twelve people seeking sanctuary, referred by local medical centres.

Claiming sanctuary in the UK can be a very isolating experience, so aside from all the other benefits of the project, it also offers a place to meet people from other communities, not just those in the same situation as themselves. Greenfingers is not a project specifically for asylum seekers and refugees, which means everyone there can benefit from the mix of cultures and backgrounds.

The project is keen to offer as much support as possible, so given the increase in the referrals of asylum seekers, they have organised a training session for the staff by the Medical Foundation for Victims of Torture. However, John Lawson, one of the project managers, explained that the fact that someone is an asylum seeker doesn't mean they need to be treated differently – they use the same supportive approach for everyone. For example, it's about knowing when to give someone a quiet space when they need it, or a shoulder to lean on.

The regularity of the sessions offers stability for people whose lives are often filled with uncertainty. In addition, the range of activities available means it's easier to find something you enjoy doing – for example, one of the members used to be a chef before he came to the UK, so now he chooses to cook the lunch for everyone, as it is something he enjoys doing, and distracts him from what's going on inside his head. The social side of Greenfingers is important, and each session they sit down for a lunch together and also go on trips occasionally. One refugee described the people there as a "family".

TWO

Sanctuary, hospitality and refuge in world faiths

The 'Sanctuary Knocker' at Durham Cathedral

The practices of sanctuary, hospitality and refuge are rooted in universal human experience. They have been taught and valued by the most ancient human societies, and continue to resonate deeply with people from many different cultures and traditions.

Exploring how different faith traditions have practised and interpreted these themes offers one way for people from different communities and backgrounds to learn from each other, on the basis of a shared concern for people seeking sanctuary today.

This chapter explores some perspectives on sanctuary, hospitality and refuge from different world faiths, Christianity, Islam, Judaism, Buddhism, the Baha'i Faith, Sikhism and Hinduism as an illustration of the different insights that diverse traditions have to share with each other. We hope that this might also encourage sharing of different faith perspectives at a local level, as in the example of the Sheffield interfaith event which is also included.

The History of Sanctuary[1]

The roots of Sanctuary are thousands of years old, and have their basis in such diverse cultures as ancient Egyptian, Hebrew and

---

1   Prof Paul Weller

Greek. The Hebrew tradition enshrined the experience of a formerly oppressed people into the legal code of their new society when six Cities of Refuge/Sanctuary were established according to the legislation set out in the Book of Numbers. These cities were able to give refuge to anyone, including a foreigner who was accused of manslaughter, thus preventing the automatic use of blood feud as a rough, ready and often indiscriminately unfair route to justice:

Then the LORD said to Moses; "Speak to the Israelites and say to them: 'When you cross the Jordan into Canaan, select some towns to be your cities of refuge, to which a person who has killed someone accidentally may flee. They will be places of refuge from the avenger, so that a person accused of murder may not die before he stands trial before the assembly... These six towns will be a refuge for Israelites, aliens and any other people living among them, so that anyone who has killed another accidentally can flee there.'" Numbers 35: 9-15

The Hebrew tradition provided the basis for the incorporation of sanctuary into the life of Western European society through its adoption by the Christian Church; and with the transition of the Church from a persecuted sect into an officially recognised and promoted religion, sanctuary became legally recognised, although always subject to certain restrictions, and often caught in the tension between the competing claims of Church and State over the boundaries of their spheres of authority.

The earliest mention of sanctuary in England was in the code of laws issued by King Aethelbert in the year 600AD. Under Norman rule, there were two kinds of sanctuary:

- a general right to sanctuary which belonged to every church
- a particular right to sanctuary which was granted to some cities by Royal Charter.

The number of sanctuaries were reduced in the reign of Henry VIII, and in 1623, the general right to sanctuary was abolished by statute law, although the basis of sanctuary has always been moral.

Christian sanctuaries, in early Church history, were for fugitive slaves. In Britain, the first Christian martyr, St Alban, was canonised because he was martyred for giving sanctuary to a fleeing person.

The concept of sanctuary re-emerged in the 20th Century, first in El Salvador, as a form of protection from the activities of 'death squads'. From there it was taken up in the USA when churches sheltered Guatemalans and Salvadorians refused asylum.

In 1982, a Presbyterian Church in Arizona, unwilling to see people sent back to certain detention, became the first Church to offer sanctuary. Scores more followed, and were joined by synagogues.

There have been sanctuaries for migrants in Germany, Switzerland, Denmark and Sweden as well as in the UK. The best known sanctuary in UK was that taken by Viraj Mendis in the Parish Church of the Ascension, Hulme, Manchester; 20th December 1986 to 18th January 1989.

A Christian reflection on Hospitality[2]

In Deuteronomy 10: 17-19, we read:

'The Lord your God is God of gods and Lord of lords, the great God, mighty and awesome, who is not partial and takes no bribe, who executes justice for the orphan and the widow, and who loves the strangers, providing them with food and clothing. You shall also love the stranger, for you were strangers in the land of Egypt.'

Why should we love the stranger? Because God loves the stranger – and, remember, 'you were strangers in the land of Egypt'. The Hebrew – the stranger in Egypt, to whom God showed love, is now required to love the stranger.

God's holiness is not seen in God's remoteness or separateness from the stranger, but by God's utter concern for the stranger, by God's adoption and embrace of the stranger. God requires nothing

---

2   Extract from a sermon by Inderjit Bhogal.

less from those who would be holy. God is outraged when 'the stranger residing among you suffers extortion' (Ezekiel 22: 7). This is the God who is seen in Jesus of Nazareth. God is the incarnate one, the one who is in our midst.

Jesus cuts through boundaries and separation between who is considered to be holy and profane. Jesus' most subversive and radical activity, for which he is most criticised, is to eat with the social outcasts of his day. It is said that 'he eats with sinners and tax collectors.' The tax collectors were not flavour of the day because they collaborated with the 'outsiders'.

Jesus expressed his solidarity with the poor and marginalised people of his day by eating with them. He welcomes the poor, 'the unclean', 'the sinners', the harlots and publicans and ate with them. In this he showed God's way, God's truth and God's life. He demonstrates a holiness of connectedness, not separateness, of intimacy, not aloofness.

Jesus
- breaks down barriers
- crosses boundaries
- includes those who would have been excluded
- eats with anyone who would eat with him.

Everything Jesus did and said demonstrated these things.

Jesus has left an example for his community. Practice hospitality. Eat with each other. Eat with the most vulnerable ones. Eat with 'the stranger.' Your lifestyle should be one of hospitality and solidarity, not hostility and segregation.

The ethics of so many are about
- Segregation
- Division
- Derision
- Hostility

They may extend to 'love of neighbour.'

The Biblical and gospel demand is for a different, counter-cultural ethic: 'God loves the stranger… you shall also love the stranger.'

The strength of this requirement is seen in the fact that it is stated 37 times in the Hebrew Bible. Jesus demonstrates the ethic of hospitality and eating with outcasts, and says that in welcoming the stranger, one welcomes Christ: 'I was a stranger and you welcomed me… truly, I tell you, just as you did it to one of the least of these… you did it to me.' (Matthew 25: 35, 40)

We are all made in the image of God. We are challenged to see the face of Christ in those in greatest need and who feel most vulnerable and powerless, and respond.

A Muslim perspective on Hospitality[3]

The Prophet Muhammad (peace be upon him) once stated that 'Islam began as a stranger and will return as a stranger, so give glad tidings to the strangers!' Islam began in a desert, semi-nomadic climate where tribalism had a strong influence on people's lives. One of the key aspects of the Prophet's struggle was to work against this tribalism in which there was little room for strangers and foreigners. In fact strangers could be harshly discriminated against, especially if they were poor. One such story shows how the prophet Muhammad, quite early in his life, stood up against injustice.

When the Prophet was in his teens, a trader from Yemen came to Makka and was wronged by one of the Makkans who bought goods from him and refused to give the agreed price. In those days people would be protected through their family or clan and, knowing that the trader had no protection, the Makkan felt that he would get away with this. The trader went to the Ka'ba (almost like a village square) and pleaded for help. In response to this a group of people met in the house of Abdullah ibn Jud'an.

Those present at the meeting formed a pact to protect the innocent and downtrodden. The Prophet, along with his close friend Abu Bakr, was a party to this pledge. Later, in old age, he

---

3   Leicester Faiths Support Group for Asylum-Seekers & Refugees.

recalled the pledge, known as the Hilf al-Fudul (the virtuous pact) with fondness and said that he was still bound by the pact.

Islam is a religion based upon equality of people regardless of colour, ethnicity or creed. Muslims believe all human beings have originated from the same source – Muhammad said 'You are all Adam's offspring and Adam was made of clay' – thus we are all brothers and sisters of one another, whether they differ in wealth, status, gender or religion the principle of dignity and respect towards other human beings is a universal one. This is not to say that all Muslims live up to this ideal, but the teachings are clear:

'O mankind! We have created you from a male and a female, and made you into nations and tribes, that you may know one another. Verily, the most honourable of you is the one who is most conscious of God. Verily, God is all-knowing, all-aware'
(Qur'an 49: 13)

Difference and diversity – especially of race and colour – are thus seen as positive characteristics of our lives, present by God's Divine intent and not by accident. This is also exemplified in the Hajj, the pilgrimage to Makkah, during which the pilgrims, whether rich or poor, king or peasant, all dress in the same simple clothes and worship side by side.

Furthermore, the kind and merciful treatment of those in need was strongly advocated by the prophet Muhammad. He said, 'Feed them with the food which you eat, clothe them with such clothing as you wear and do not cause trouble to God's creatures.' The Prophet Muhammad's traditions also mention how on the Day of Judgement, God will say to someone 'O son of Adam, I fell ill and you visited Me not'. The response shall be: 'O Lord, how could I visit You when You are the Lord of the worlds?' God will say: 'Did you not know that so-and-so had fallen ill and you visited him not? Had you visited him you would have found Me with him'. And likewise God will ask about people who were hungry and thirsty.

Similar teachings can be located regarding the rights of neighbours, regardless of faith. 'He is not a true Muslim, who eats his fill while his neighbour sleeps on an empty stomach,' said the Prophet.

It can be seen from these teachings that it is the responsibility of a Muslim to look out for and take care of those in less fortunate circumstances on the basis of human equality.

A Baha'i Reflection on Hospitality[4]

All the founders of faiths themselves suffered oppression, such as Christ and Mohammed, yet they advocated kindness to strangers and love for humanity. Displaced from their country or cities, refugees face persecution because of their race, nationality, politics or religion. The Baha'i writings advocate hospitality and compassion in words such as, 'when a man turns his face to God he finds sunshine everywhere. All men are his brothers… Be kind to strangers, whether they come from Turkey, Japan, Persia, Russia, China or any other country in the world. Help to make them feel at home.' (Abdu'l Baha, 'Paris Talks')

Baha'u'llah, whose name means 'The Glory of God' in Arabic, was the founder of the Baha'i faith. Born on November 12th in Tehran, Iran, He did not seek political position or power, despite coming from a noble family close to the royal family, and expectations that He might take up a position at court. Instead He was known as The Father of the Poor, a 'refuge for every weak one, a shelter for every fearing one, kind to everyone, lenient and loving to all creatures.' Generosity and hospitality characterised His relationships with the poor.

Accused of a crime he had not committed and of which He was entirely innocent, Baha'u'llah was taken into Tehran's 'Black Pit' prison, an underground dungeon, dark and rancid. For three days Baha'u'llah was placed in stocks and forced to wear a hundred pound iron chain around his neck. Whilst facing these terrible conditions in this prison for four months, He received a Revelation from God. 'I was a man like others, asleep upon My couch, when lo, the breezes of the All-Glorious were wafted over Me, and taught Me the knowledge of all that hath been.' This marked the start of a flowing ocean of Divine Revelation.

4   Leicester Faiths Support Group for Asylum-Seekers & Refugees.

These new teachings advocated:

- an independent search for truth
- the oneness of God and humanity
- harmony between science and religion
- eliminating extremes of wealth and poverty
- the equality of men and women
- universal education for all
- the eradication of all prejudice, and seeking work to serve and benefit humanity

These teachings started spreading rapidly throughout the Persian Empire, and as a result Baha'u'llah and his family faced banishment. This period from 1852 onwards marked the start of forty years of exile to Iraq, Turkey and Palestine, combined with further imprisonment and persecution.

Abdu'l Baha, the son of Baha'u'llah, was the perfect example of what a true Baha'i should be. He gave to the poor and knew them personally, able to make enquiries after their families. Regularly he sent food, clothing and medicine to those in need. Therefore, his actions were in harmony with his words. 'Be ye loving fathers to the orphan, and a refuge to the helpless, and a treasury for the poor, and a cure for the ailing. Be ye the helpers of every victim of oppression, the patrons of the disadvantaged. Think ye at all times of rendering service to every member of the human race… Let him do some good to every person whose path he crosseth, and be of some benefit to him.' (Abdu'l Baha, Selections from the Writings of Abdu'l Baha)

There is no limit to human potential and often those who have suffered the most have been able to contribute the most to society. Therefore we must actively allow others to realise their great destiny. In the words of Abdu'l Baha, 'do not be content with showing friendship in words alone, let your heart burn with loving kindness for all who may cross your path.'

'Every person has a valuable contribution to make to society.'

'The Earth is but one country and mankind its citizens', and 'We are the leaves of one tree and the flowers of one garden.'

A Sikh Reflection on Hospitality[5]

Compassion and service to the community is ingrained in the Sikh psyche by the teaching of the ten Gurus, which are enshrined in the Sikh Holy Scripture – Sri Guru Granth Sahib Jee. To illustrate this way of life, below are a few stories.

Guru Nanak even at a very early age would show compassion to those who were shunned by society, like the poor and untouchables. One of the famous stories of his life includes the business trip he was sent on by his father Metha Kalu to bring some goods back to sell. However, on his way the Guru met a group of faqirs (ascetics) who were hungry for several days. The Guru spent all the money in feeding the faqirs and called it a true bargain. Obviously he didn't complete the job his father wanted him to but his nature was to help the poor and hungry.

One of the most famous stories in Sikh history, which illustrates a great sacrifice in the aid of refugees and asylum seekers, is that of the Martyrdom of the ninth Guru, Sri Guru Tegh Bahadur Sahib Jee.

A delegation of 500 Kashmiri Brahmins led by Pandit Kirpa Ram came to seek refuge and protection from Guru Teg Bahadur Jee at Anandpur Sahib. Pandit Kirpa Ram told the harrowing tales of torture initiated by the orders of Aurangzeb (r. 1658-1707 AD) for converting them to Islam.

Guru Jee was mentally occupied with the issue when the child Gobind Rai happened to be there and asked as to what was the matter. Guru Jee told him that the sacrifice of a Great Soul is called for. 'Who else than you can serve this cause?' was the child Gobind Rai's spontaneous reaction. Thus Guru Jee was martyred as he refused to convert to Islam. The story here should show that the help offered to the Kashmiri Pandits by Guru Jee was the ultimate assistance anyone could give to another human being, that is his own life.

5   Leicester Faiths Support Group for Asylum-Seekers & Refugees.

To sum up, the teachings of the Sikh religion ultimately tell us to offer assistance to anyone less fortunate than ourselves. To show compassion to those in need and offer them the help they need to get back on their feet. However, Guru Nanak laid forth three basic principles by which every human being should abide:

1. Remember the name of God at all times.
2. Earn an honest living as a householder.
3. Share a portion of your earnings and time to help the less fortunate.

As a Sikh, we should live according to these rules, and the best way to help asylum seekers is to help them to help themselves. The label of a refugee and asylum seeker can be disabling to many, however if one helps them to become a contributing member of society that can be of more help than one can envisage, and change that person's life totally around.

A Buddhist reflection on Refuge and Generosity[6]

'Aware of suffering caused by exploitation, social injustice, stealing and oppression, I am committed to cultivating loving kindness and learning ways to work for the wellbeing of people, animals, plants and minerals. I will practise generosity by sharing my time, energy and material resources with those who are in real need. I am determined not to steal and not to possess anything that should belong to others. I will respect the property of others, but I will prevent others from profiting from human suffering or the suffering of other species on Earth.'

Second mindfulness training of the Community of Interbeing

'Subhuti, if a bodhisattva does not rely on anything when practising generosity, then the happiness that results from that virtue is as great as space.' *Diamond Sutra*

'Oh Blessed One, may I not come to the complete awakening if, when I have done so, there should, in my Pure Land, be any

6   Gina Clayton

discrimination of regard or privilege between humans and devas or between different individuals on such grounds as colour, relative beauty or other criteria, save the harmless kind of discrimination that is necessary for naming and keeping count of things.'

Dharmakara's fourth vow, from the Larger Pureland Sutra

The *second mindfulness training from the Community of Interbeing*, which is set out here, is an inspiring contemporary elaboration of the second precept in Buddhism: to not take what is not given – or one might say, not to steal. This is very relevant to creating a City of Sanctuary because it rests on the central insight of Buddhism, the realisation that everything is dependent on something else – or really on many other things.

From this point of view, there is no 'my city' or 'my home' in a way that gives me exclusive rights over it. There is only the recognition that I benefit from all the people and other conditions (like the sun and the rain) that have created my present life. We vow to 'not take what is not given' not really because something is 'mine' or 'yours' but rather because if I take what is not given to me I am acting out of an unworthy motive such as greed. In doing that I undermine relationship; I do not fully respect the other and create less good conditions immediately for myself and others. There is no cause to elevate myself and my own needs over others, because whatever I am is only to a small extent of my own doing.

This leads to it being a natural and right thing to share the benefits of the world. Generosity is one of the six virtues in Buddhism, but at root there is not a sharp distinction between the giver and the receiver. There is a belief that giving or sharing, as an activity, creates good energy, and that good energy is meant to be given away. So giving or sharing, including in particular sharing the pleasure one has in giving – which means allowing and enabling others to give – is an essential building block in creating what a Buddhist might call a 'pure land' or a 'field of merit'. These are the kinds of places people like to live – where there is happiness. So it is a pleasure and a privilege to have the opportunity to give or to share.

The extract from the Larger Pureland Sutra also points to the Buddhist teaching of fundamental spiritual equality. Even though some people have greater accomplishments than others, we often cannot even see clearly what is great and what is not. At root there is equality between all beings. This is demonstrated in a well known teaching of the Buddha called the Karaniya Metta Sutta:

Think of every being without exception: the weak and the strong, from the smallest to the largest, whether you can see them or not, beings living now or yet to arise – may all beings become happy in their heart of hearts.

Refuge is a central idea in Buddhism. If a person wants formally to 'become a Buddhist' they go through a ceremony in which they 'take refuge' in Buddha, Dharma and Sangha. Even without such formality, taking refuge can be a moment-to-moment intention or act of entrusting oneself to the Buddha and the Buddha's teaching. Taking refuge is not a flight from the world. It is based on a recognition that we all take refuge – i.e. put our trust in – something, and it is an invitation to put our trust in something that is worthy of that trust. It is not a 'refuge from' but a 'refuge in'. Buddhists recognise that that act of taking refuge, of putting our trust in something, is a fundamental need for human beings.

Putting these ideas together, from a Buddhist perspective, creating a City of Sanctuary is about creating the conditions which are closer to conditions of trustworthiness and ultimate good for everyone, and it is about being grateful for the opportunity to recognise that what I have is not 'mine' and to share it.

A Hindu Reflection on Sanctuary[7]

Oneness amongst people, the advancement of unity in diversity is the core of Hindu religion. This religion has taught the world both tolerance and universal acceptance. We believe not only in universal toleration, but we accept all religion as true.

India has sheltered the persecuted and the refugees of all religions and all nations of the earth. India has gathered in her bosom the

7   Dr Vithal Patel

purest remnants of Israelites, who came to southern India and took refuge in the very year in which their holy temple was shattered to pieces by Roman tyranny. Similarly India sheltered and is still fostering the remnant of the grand Zoroastrian nation. When Mohamed started Islam in 600 AD Arabs invaded Persia which is now called Iran. At that time Zoroastrians were living happily in Iran. Arabs tried to convert them to Islam or kill the men and kidnap the women. Zoroastrians, now called Parsi, were the most peaceful and intelligent race in Iran. To avoid atrocity they sailed away from Iran to India and landed in Gujarat.

There is an interesting story for all asylum seekers and fostered people to learn. The Zoroastrians' leader requested the king Rana of Gujarat to settle in his part of the country. To this the king answered them with a full glass of milk, suggesting that we are full and can not accommodate any more population. The Parsi leader replied by adding sugar in the milk and requested the king to taste it. They have settled in the country like sweet milk, without causing any harm and merged with the local population and helped progress in the country. The examples are Tata who owns Corus and car industries, and Bhabha who helped in atomic energy in India. The moral to learn from this is to be faithful to the adopted and fostered country and follow the rule of the country.

A Hindu is one who believes in the basic principles of Hinduism and applies them to everyday life. Basically they are as follows:

1. There is one God, who has become everything in this universe. This implies that everyone and everything has to be considered with due regard. This talks about the basic unity of the whole universe. This implies that one has to strive for the welfare of the whole. There is no place for selfishness or narrowness.

2. The aim of life is to realise God. There is no room for desultory living. Life has a great divine purpose. It is to overcome all limitations by realizing the divinity within.

3. Every path to God is true. Everyone has to choose a path to God according to one's own temperament. There is no conflict between various religions.

If one follows these principles, one is a Hindu. It does not matter whether you worship Krishna or Christ or Allah. Mahatma Gandhi said "I consider myself a Hindu, Christian, Muslim, Jew, Buddhist and Confucian."

Hinduism is a philosophy that believes in three main principles.

1. Atma - Eternal spirit

2. Karma - Action of deeds

3. Rebirth - Reincarnation

The principle of the Hindu religion is Ahinsha (Non violence or do not hurt or kill anybody) and Shanti (Peace). A Hindu believes in Peace which is an art. We learn this from the nature created by God. It does not differentiate race, religion, sex or colour. Nobel Prize winner Ravindranath Tagore once said, "The world is my school and the nature is my book." Nature can not be changed. Sun rises from east and sets in west. This can not be changed. What is changed is human mind. Good, bad and ugly thought creates action accordingly. War and fanaticism are the primitive action of the society. The human civilisation has advanced very much. We have reached the Moon and Mars. Primitivism is static, stops the progress of human being. We should give up primitive ideas and help the next generation to preserve nature and progress forward. It is not too late to act in peaceful faith. There is a verse in the Bible "Hope deferred maketh the heart sick, but when the desire of peace is come to pass, the heart rejoiceth." May it be so for all of us.

We teach our children five principles.

1. Respect women - the important members of the family who brought us into the world.

2. Respect elders and learn wisdom from their experience.

3. Tolerance to other religions.

4. All living things are important.

5. Extended family to look after each other.

A Hindu prays to God for providing the five essentials for life-Earth, Air, Fire, Water and Sky. We call it the 'Panch Bhoota' without which the universe can not exist.

The chanting of mantras grants us the wisdom, the glow on our face and longevity. The Mantra in Sanskrit is "Om Bhoorbuvastvaha Tatsavithur virenyam. Bhargo devasya dheemahi, diyoyona prachodyat." (Oh creator of universe! We meditate upon thy supreme splendour. May thy radiant power illuminate our intellect, destroy our sins and guide us in the right direction.)

We are all children of God. We hope to live in peace and harmony by respecting each other.

The Terminus Initiative, Sheffield

Photo: Banner made by women at the Conversation Club

The first time Joy Adams ever met someone she knew to be an asylum seeker was when a young woman from West Africa came to the church where Joy was giving a sermon. The experience opened her eyes to the realities of what people seeking sanctuary in the UK face.

Joy was already involved in a project called the Terminus Initiative, set up in 2002 by four local churches on a housing estate in a disadvantaged area of the city. Among other activities the project runs a local café offering healthy food at a reasonable price. There are a small number of asylum seekers housed in this area, and because there are so few, it can be a very isolating experience for them.

The Terminus Initiative began its involvement with people seeking sanctuary through running a Women's Conversation Club for women of any background wishing to practice their English in a friendly and safe environment. The Terminus Café is run by volunteers, and the progression to involving people seeking sanctuary as volunteers was quite organic – some came from the Conversation Club, some from local churches, and others had simply found out about the café online.

Joy doesn't feel it is useful to differentiate between people, and they treat everyone as equal at the café. Furthermore, Joy doesn't feel that involving people seeking sanctuary has caused them any more work, as all the volunteers come with their own individual needs. For example, communication difficulties can arise for a number of reasons, not just because English is not someone's first language.

A real benefit for the people from refugee backgrounds who volunteer at the café is that they feel more of the community, and they are a part of something where they feel needed. It is also a positive experience for people from the "host" community to meet the individuals behind the labels of "asylum seeker" or "refugee".

For any organisation thinking of involving people seeking sanctuary in their work, Joy does give one piece of advice, which is to be prepared to get drawn in. "It's not the sort of work that you can just fiddle about with. It has to be done properly." After all, the people you are involving are often in a very vulnerable situation and could feel let down. She notes that it is also very difficult to do on your own, as you will probably get emotionally involved. But, she says, there is information and support available, so look out for what is there. For Joy, she first felt anger at the injustices which were happening, but now she has a way of channelling it into something more beneficial.

Sanctuary, Hospitality and Refuge Event
Sheffield, December 2007

Photo: Zeela Gospel choir

The aims of the event were to:

- Hear the stories of people seeking sanctuary in our city
- Share participants' own experiences of sanctuary and welcome
- Explore what sanctuary, hospitality and refuge mean to people of different faiths
- Learn how faith communities can make their city a more welcoming place for people seeking sanctuary.

There were 50 participants from the Buddhist, Muslim, Anglican, Catholic, Methodist, Seventh Day Adventist, Quaker, Jewish, Humanist and Unitarian traditions.

Following a brief introduction by representatives of Sheffield Faiths Forum and City of Sanctuary, Christian and Muslim refugees shared their experiences of arriving in Sheffield. They stressed the importance of the welcome and support they had received from local faith groups and how this had affected their own faith, particularly meeting and working with people of different faiths.

Members of Sheffield faith communities then gave short readings and commentary about the concepts of sanctuary, hospitality and welcome from the Jewish, Islamic and Buddhist traditions. This was followed by a performance from the Zeela Gospel Choir – part of the Liberian community in Sheffield. A large part of the evening was given to conversation and sharing of experiences by the participants. At tables during the buffet, the following questions were discussed:

What do sanctuary / hospitality / refuge mean to me and my faith?

When have I felt welcome or unwelcome in a community?

What relationships do I and my faith community have with asylum-seekers and refugees?

Feedback from the tables was collected and there were contributions from a wide variety of participants including the Karen community from Burma.

As a direct result of the event members of one faith community were able to offer accommodation to someone who was homeless as a result of being refused sanctuary.

Muslim Welfare House of Sheffield

The Muslim Welfare House of Sheffield (MWHS) for many years has been a centre for all. By "all", we mean those who are prosperous and those who are not so. This includes those who have settled down to life in Britain and those who have travelled many miles seeking asylum and refuge in Britain; because they feel that Britain will offer them security and a chance for a better life. By "all" we mean all races and backgrounds.

The Muslim Welfare House is just as the name applies: It is run by Muslims and offers Welfare to those who are in need. And because of this the MWHS has been catering for asylum seekers in many ways. In the month of Ramadan, for instance, the month of extended generosity, the MWHS invites all to come and share in the breakfast meal at sunset. During the Eid, the time of festival, all are invited to participate in the celebrations.

Amongst all this, the MWHS has a hardship fund. Although limited in resources, it aims to help those who are in need, to get them through the difficult times, until they can get on their feet. Using money that others give in the way of Zakat (compulsory charity that a Muslim pays) to finance this hardship fund.

With more than 45 different nationalities attending the MWHS, the very nature of the broad spectrum of the worshippers at the MWHS allows anyone to come and feel welcomed and not a stranger. And this in itself is a service which promotes emotional comfort and support for the refugees who find themselves isolated and lonely.

The Muslim Welfare House has also provided accommodation to one asylum-seeker and now he has managed to complete his PhD from Sheffield University.

THREE

Giving a City of Sanctuary talk

What's your Audience?

It's helpful to think in advance about what sort of audience you will have, and to tailor your talk to their concerns and experiences. You are likely to have a different reception from an Amnesty International group, compared with a local tenants' association or Rotary Club, for example.

It may be helpful to consider some of the different types of people who might make up your audience, and the kinds of information that will be relevant and convincing to them. In his book 'Carbon Detox', environmental campaigner George Marshall illustrates different approaches to communicating with four groups, which he calls 'survivors', 'traditionalists', 'winners' and 'strivers'.

Survivors' main focus is on coping with their own lives. They are likely to have anxieties about competition for scarce resources such as housing, jobs etc. In relation to City of Sanctuary, the main message for survivors is that refugees can be good for their communities; that they generally come from traditional societies where people look out for their neighbours. It may be good to illustrate this with examples of how refugees have made friends with their neighbours and have been able to help them out with babysitting, studying together etc.

Traditionalists are concerned with upholding traditional values, such as community, religion and family. They may be older people, and may have concerns about people seeking sanctuary being criminals, contributing to overpopulation, or eroding traditional British society. For this group it is useful to emphasise that offering sanctuary is an important tradition of our society, and that it is central to Christian and other faiths. You may want to use examples of how refugees have contributed positively to their communities, for example reviving some dwindling Church congregations, working in care homes, doing voluntary work for charities etc. This group is very concerned with fairness, so it may also be helpful to refer to many refugees' strong motivation to work hard and provide a safe and peaceful future for their families.

Winners are mainly focused on personal success, and getting the most out of life for themselves. They may be younger people, and are less swayed by ethical arguments. It may be most helpful to refer to the cultural assets that refugees bring to Britain, including music, food, fashion etc, and how much less interesting it would be without them.

Strivers are people who want to live ethically and make the world a better place. This is your most likely audience of 'natural supporters' in refugee and human rights organisations. Strivers will be motivated by the ethical appeal and vision of City of Sanctuary. They will want to know how City of Sanctuary is going to make a real difference to refugees, and may need convincing about the importance of trying to work with the City Council, police etc, rather than adopting a more confrontational approach.

Keep it Personal

The most convincing speakers are those who communicate their own enthusiasm for their subject, sharing their own experiences rather than just dry packages of information.

It is very helpful to use some of your own personal stories to illustrate why you are supporting City of Sanctuary and what friendship with people seeking sanctuary means to you. This will help the audience to connect much more strongly with your message.

Craig Barnett has told several groups the story of his mother, who was a young girl in Liverpool during World War 2. When her house was bombed, (with her inside it, but unharmed underneath the stairs) she was evacuated to Wales, where she spent the rest of the war. He tells them how his mother's experience has helped her to identify with people seeking sanctuary in Britain, and that she sometimes asks him, 'how are your evacuees getting on?'

He uses this story as a reminder that it is not so long ago that many of our own families needed a place of safety, and how some of us perhaps are only alive because others offered them sanctuary. Any personal story of your own will help to keep your audience interested and engaged; it could be the story of a friendship with a refugee, or an event that has touched or motivated you in some way.

Powerpoint

Try to avoid using Powerpoint presentations. These can work well if you have some good photos or video to add to your talk, and if you can manage to avoid turning round to face the screen. Otherwise, Powerpoint slides which just summarise the points of a talk are a distraction for audiences and speaker. It is much more important to make eye contact with listeners and to avoid fiddling with a computer.

For the same reason it is deadly to read your talk aloud from a printed page. Reading out written English is also very different from the kind of language used in normal conversations, which tends to distance listeners further. It is much more effective to note down your key points on one piece of paper or on index cards, so that you can instantly remind yourself of your next point, and then return your attention to your audience as you speak. It takes practice to get used to speaking in a natural way to groups. It is often helpful to try your talks out several times by yourself, and then to a friend or family members, until you get used to it.

Terminology

Try to avoid using jargon words and expressions such as 'social cohesion', 'NGOs', 'outcomes', 'voluntary and community sector' etc. There may be some audiences of specialists who will respond to these buzz-words, but in general such abstract language tends to distance listeners and is best avoided in favour of concrete and everyday English. It is much more vivid and immediate to talk about 'how people get on together' rather than 'community cohesion'.

There is a similar problem with the term 'asylum-seeker', which has a technical meaning understood by refugee professionals, but for the general public is synonymous with 'illegal immigrants' and criminality in general. On the basis of its research into public attitudes, the Independent Asylum Commission has concluded that talking about 'asylum-seekers' creates a barrier to thinking about the issues of forced migration, which most people don't associate with the expression.

The IAC recommends that we should avoid using this expression when trying to communicate with the general public, and instead talk about people seeking sanctuary, which is a word that people do associate with the need for safety and protection. Of course with refugee professionals and others who use it as a technical term it will be more relevant to talk about asylum-seekers. Our 'welcome' sign also refers to 'asylum-seekers and refugees', as it offers a more explicit challenge to hostile stereotypes and will also be easily recognised by people seeking sanctuary themselves.

Key points for your talk

1. History

The City of Sanctuary movement started in Sheffield in October 2005, from a meeting of some of the people supporting refugees in the city, to explore the idea of a positive vision for Sheffield as a place of welcome and safety.

Participants at that meeting went back to the groups that they had contacts with, to ask them to pass official resolutions of support for becoming a City of Sanctuary, which included a commitment to welcome and include refugees and asylum-seekers in their own activities.

Our aim was to build up enough grassroots support to eventually persuade the City Council to offer their support. By June 2007, we had over 70 supporting organisations in Sheffield, and the Council approached us to offer their endorsement, with cross-party support.

Since our official launch as the UK's first City of Sanctuary in September 2007, the idea has spread across the UK. Just a year after Sheffield's launch there were already 9 cities with active City of Sanctuary groups.

It's helpful to give your audience a sense that their participation in the City of Sanctuary movement is of historical importance. At significant events like launches of local City of Sanctuary groups, we congratulate people on being present, telling them it is something they will look back on and be proud to have been there.

At our first national conference in 2008, Donna Covey, Chief Executive of the Refugee Council, described City of Sanctuary as a 'once in a generation opportunity' to change how the UK welcomes people seeking sanctuary. By supporting their local City of Movement, the group you are speaking to can make a contribution to this change.

You could mention other recent developments in the national network, upcoming launches or successes, which all give a sense of the movement's dynamism and significance.

2. Vision

City of Sanctuary offers a vision of a town or city that is safe and welcoming to people in need of sanctuary, and that gives them a chance to contribute their skills and gifts to the whole community. This is something that everyone in the city can work towards and be proud of.

A city that welcomes people in need of safety is a better place for everyone, because it will be more welcoming, more accepting of difference, and it will also benefit from the active participation of people from different cultures and backgrounds.

Much 'awareness-raising' about refugees focuses on the hardships, sufferings and injustices that they face. It is important to make people aware of the injustices of the current asylum system (arbitrary and indefinite detention, destitution, removal of right to work etc), but our focus is on a positive vision of what kind of city and country we want to be, rather than just being 'against' the current government. We also want to give people opportunities to get to know refugees not just as 'victims', but as real people with gifts and experiences to contribute to their communities.

3. Action

It's important to be clear about what you want your audience to do as a result of your talk. In general, we want organisations to pass a formal resolution of support for their local City of Sanctuary movement. As part of this, we also want them to make a concrete decision about how they will be more inclusive of people seeking sanctuary, for example by advertising their activities to refugee communities, making links with other organisations, offering volunteer placements etc.

We also want supporters to help City of Sanctuary to grow by talking to other groups they are involved with about it. They can also sign up to receive our email newsletter by giving you their email address.

Hostile questions

Although audiences generally respond positively to the City of Sanctuary message, there can be individuals who express anger or hostility, and it is good to be prepared with a strategy for responding to this. One very powerful and simple technique is called 'Nonviolent Communication' or NVC. For our purposes, the key steps of NVC are as follows:

1. Don't focus on the opinions being expressed, instead listen for the feelings and needs behind what they are saying.

2. Check that you have understood the feeling and the need by asking 'Are you feeling… because you want….'

3. When the person knows that their feelings and needs have been heard and understood by you, they will be ready to hear about your feelings, needs and values.

Eg: *'Why are you so concerned about all these bogus asylum-seekers coming halfway around the world to claim our benefits, when our own pensioners can't afford to keep warm? Why aren't you doing something for the people who've lived here all their lives instead of all these illegal immigrants who are just on the make.'*

It will not help to explain to this person that asylum-seekers can't claim benefits, or the difference between an asylum-seeker and an illegal immigrant, until they feel that their anger has been heard and acknowledged. Eg:

Speaker: *'Are you angry because you want British pensioners to have enough money to live on?'*

Audience member: *'It's a disgrace, spending all this money on immigrants, you lot can't do enough for them, but what are you doing for people from round here?'*

Speaker: *'Do you feel outraged that local people aren't being treated fairly?'*

It is not necessary to respond to the beliefs or opinions expressed at this stage, just to let the other person know that their feelings have been heard. This may take a while, but once they know that you have heard and understood them you will have an opportunity to share your own point of view, including your own feelings.

Speaker: *'I want local people to be treated fairly too, and I feel angry that some pensioners can't afford their bills. I also want us to treat people fairly who have had to come here to keep their families safe. I want us to try to work together to make this city a better place for everybody to live in.'*

Supporters of refugees have also occasionally made hostile comments, taking out their anger at the injustice of the system on us for not criticising the Council and the government strongly enough. It is possible to simply acknowledge that anger, and share your own feelings about the way refugees are treated, and what you are trying to do about it. This has been enough to completely alter an aggressive encounter into a sense of shared purpose.

There is more on NVC in Marshall Rosenberg's book 'Nonviolent Communication', or at www.cnvc.org

FOUR

Organising a City of Sanctuary public event

Public events are a chance for City of Sanctuary supporters to meet each other, and for refugees and local people to make contact and share experiences. They are also an opportunity to celebrate your achievements and communicate your vision to potential new supporters.

Launch events

Most groups have created a public launch event early in their initiative, to gather and motivate potential supporters. For these events to work, it is vital that they are enjoyable, creative, and leave people feeling enthusiastic and clear about how they can get involved. Bear in mind that many of the people you want to involve will already be active in many different groups. They will need to feel that their local City of Sanctuary initiative won't be just another round of dutifully attending meetings, but is something they will enjoy and be energised by. Your events are also an opportunity to motivate people who may not have been involved in community projects before. The more original and inspiring you can make the event, the more likely they will be to take part. You only get to launch once, so it is worth giving it plenty of thought and preparation.

This is an opportunity to invite people who are active in local community organisations and networks, and those with contacts in different sectors, such as business, the police, schools, universities, and local government, as well as refugee communities and organisations. Many groups have also invited high profile guests such as faith leaders, local Councillors, and the Mayor.

It is often possible to use existing networks such as Voluntary Action, faith forums, and regeneration agencies to help publicise your launch, and reach the widest possible audience. It is also worth thinking about using social networking tools such as Facebook, as well as local radio, newspapers and television.

A successful launch event will be a combination of informing participants about the aims and vision of City of Sanctuary, creating space for people to share their ideas, and providing ways for them to get involved. It is important that people seeking sanctuary are involved in running the event, and active in the movement from the beginning. For many of the local people who get involved in the City of Sanctuary movement it is the opportunity to meet and talk to refugees directly that has motivated them most. A speaker who can talk briefly about their own experience of claiming sanctuary in your town or city can be a powerful part of a launch event. This should be someone who has been fully involved in the discussions around City of Sanctuary, so that their message reflects the core principles of the movement.

Elements of a launch event:

Celebration
It is good to set the atmosphere for the event with an element of music or dance by refugee artists (or a mixed local and refugee group). At the launch of Bradford City of Sanctuary, Ben Musanzi from the Democratic Republic of Congo opened the evening with a lively drumming session, explaining that 'In Africa, unless there are drums it is not a celebration.'

Speaker

It is essential to communicate your vision for your place as a City of Sanctuary (see previous chapter). At this stage though, it is enough to share the broad vision and approach, rather than going into great detail. Everyone has a limit to the amount of time they can happily sit listening to a speaker. Sitting through a whole series of speeches can be frustrating and de-energising. Try to limit the speaking element to 20 minutes or so, and then give space for people to digest and respond to what they have heard.

Discussion

There are basically two ways of having a period for discussion. One approach is to have a space for questions following the talk. In this case it is a good idea to have a short 'buzz' period first when you ask people to turn to a neighbour and take a few minutes each to share their responses to what they have heard. This gets ideas flowing and makes people more ready with questions and comments when you call for an open discussion. It's worthwhile having something loud (bell, gong, glass-and-spoon) to attract people's attention at the end.

An open discussion period can work well as long as the group is not too large. It is vulnerable, though, to being dominated by the voluble or eccentric participant who wants to use it as a platform for their strongly-held views. In this situation it is important that you have a facilitator who can firmly but politely ask people to make space for others to speak.

With groups of more than 30 or so it is preferable to organize small discussion groups. These work best with between 4 to 6 people. It is usually easiest for people to organise themselves into groups with their immediate neighbours. For some events you may want to create themed discussion groups on particular topics. For this you simply designate a different area of the room for each discussion subject, perhaps writing the topic on a sheet on the wall, and people choose the place they are interested in.

A 'world café' approach allows people to move from table to table at set intervals, so that they get to discuss several questions or topics with a different mix of people. There should always be one facilitator at each table who stays to share the results of previous conversations. There is more information on running world café events at: www.theworldcafe.com

Discussion groups need a fair amount of time, perhaps 20-40 minutes depending on how much they have to discuss. It is usually helpful to give groups one or more questions to consider, which should be as clear and simple as possible (to avoid them using the whole time discussing what the question means). You may want to give each group a piece of paper and pen and ask them to record their ideas. Tell people what the finish time is and be ready with your gong etc. It is helpful to give a couple of minutes' warning before the time is up so they can finish their conversation comfortably.

The kind of questions you might ask people to consider at a launch event include:

'What might make it difficult for people seeking sanctuary to participate in your organisation?'

'What can your organisation/local community do to help people seeking sanctuary to feel welcome and involved?'

'What could your organisation/ community do to support people seeking sanctuary in your city?'

'What can you do personally to encourage your organisation/community to take these steps?'

At Swansea's launch event, participants were grouped according to the kind of organisation they were involved with (service providers, faith, local government etc), and each group included a facilitator and at least one person seeking sanctuary, who could offer first-hand experience.

There is a tendency for discussions like this to generate lots of enthusiastic ideas about what 'someone' ought to be doing. The challenge for facilitators is to keep bringing this back to what participants can do; either themselves, by working within their own organisations, or in partnership with other groups.

After the small group discussion it is important to have a feedback session when someone from each group reports back briefly on their discussion and conclusions.

Following the discussion, collect written notes from the discussion groups, and have some way for participants to indicate how they will follow-up the suggestions made, eg by filling in a form with the actions they will take next. The Bradford launch used cut-out paper leaf shapes for written responses, which participants fixed to a wooden stand to make an 'ideas tree'.

This is an opportunity to state clearly what the next steps will be, eg volunteering to form sub-groups around specific areas of work (publicity, events, volunteering, fundraising etc) or a follow-up event or activity. Make sure that you have collected participants' (legible) email addresses. This is also a good time to make sure that everyone has one or more 'pledge of support' forms to take back to their own organisations, or to pass on to their contacts. You can encourage people to follow up on their next steps by sending out the list of action points to attenders by email after the event.

Publicity

A launch event is a perfect opportunity to start some media interest in your City of Sanctuary initiative. Local press and radio will be interested in covering your event, so contact them in advance with brief information about the event in the form of a simple press release, including a contact phone number. It's often useful to call a day or two in advance of the event too, as a reminder. If you can cultivate a relationship with one or two local journalists, this will be useful to you in the future.

It is also important to record your events with your own photographs, and if possible on video too. If you can send the local paper a good quality picture soon after an event they will be much more likely to publish a story about it. Photos are also useful for posting on your section of the City of Sanctuary website, and you can also post short clips of video or audio recordings to liven it up further.

Other public events

City of Sanctuary groups have experimented with a wide variety of public events to bring local people and people seeking sanctuary together, to raise awareness about refugee issues, and to celebrate the movement's achievements and milestones.

One of Sheffield's first events was a Ceilidh dance at a community hall, which brought people seeking sanctuary together with a wide range of local people who they wouldn't otherwise meet, in a wonderfully informal and participative way as they danced together. It was also a way to share some of Britain's indigenous culture with people from other parts of the world. One of the refugees present said, 'I never knew that Britain has its own culture too…'

Other events have included presentations by refugee speakers about their experiences of claiming sanctuary in the UK, public meetings about access to health care and the situation of unaccompanied young people claiming sanctuary, concerts by refugee musicians and drama productions by local refugee groups. The theatre group 'Actors for Human Rights' also offers performances by professional actors of productions based on the testimony of people seeking sanctuary. They are available to perform free in community venues anywhere in the country, and are a valuable resource for City of Sanctuary groups. More information at: www.iceandfire.co.uk/afhr

Another approach is a 'life swap' event, which involves people from different backgrounds who live in the same area in an evening of 'speed cultural exchange'. These events take place in a relaxed social atmosphere with food, and participants receive a 'conversation menu' of things to share about themselves in pairs – 'something I enjoy doing', 'someone I worry about' etc, before moving round to a new partner (as with 'speed dating'). This can be a rewarding way of creating real connections between people in the same neighbourhood who may not otherwise meet.

Parties are also important for celebrating anniversaries and other important milestones for your initiative. At our first anniversary party for Sheffield City of Sanctuary, we invited supporters from all over the city to an evening of African dance and drumming, music from a women's community choir and a Balkan folk band, and drama by Actors for Human Rights. We also presented City of Sanctuary awards to people seeking sanctuary for their contribution to Sheffield, and to some of the local people who have done most to make Sheffield a welcoming city.

This party didn't cost us anything. The venue was provided free and all of the artists performed without charge, and we took donations for drinks and snacks which raised several hundred pounds. It brought together an incredibly diverse group of people, of all ages, nationalities, faiths and abilities, and made a visible expression of City of Sanctuary's vision of a place of welcome and sharing.

'Stories of Sanctuary' Event, Bradford February 2009

This event enabled members of the public to hear at first hand the stories of people who have sought sanctuary in Bradford. Seven people told their stories of what had led them to flee their home countries and seek sanctuary in Bradford – stories of loss of homes, families and livelihoods, stories of rape and sexual trafficking. Each told of the battles they had fought, and in some cases are still fighting, to get the Home Office to believe their accounts, but also of their longing to use their gifts, education and experiences to benefit others.

Four of the speakers, from Iran, Congo, Nigeria and Pakistan, shared their stories 'live', and three told them anonymously via a DVD presentation (videos showing the backs of their heads and hands only).

We also wanted the evening to create a relaxed opportunity, over a free meal and through music and dance at the end, for people to meet and mingle who would not normally encounter each other. We had a Zimbabwean choir, some African drumming and song, plus an impromptu Kurdish rap at the end! Another aim was to raise awareness of, and hopefully support for, the six local voluntary groups working with those seeking sanctuary. A representative from each group briefly told the story of how they had come into being and described their vision. Some also had displays in the hall.

The venue was a spacious, but rather shabby church hall. It was chosen for its proximity to the city centre, which meant only one bus ticket each way for most people. More importantly, it is where the weekly refugee drop-in takes place, so is easy for most people to find. It is also free!

120 people attended the event and we have had a huge amount of feedback. An unexpected message that came back was how helpful many of those seeking sanctuary found it to hear others' stories. One speaker did however say that he did not have enough time to tell his story properly. This is very important and we would have fewer speakers next time. Unfortunately, we forgot to have a sign-up list for people to leave their contact details and how they could get involved in future.

We paid a professional photographer to cover the evening, and as a result now have got some great images we can use for publicity and fundraising bids. We also paid for a decent PA system.

The local paper carried a good (but not entirely accurate) article about the event, and two local radio stations broadcast interviews in advance.

FIVE

Building a local City of Sanctuary initiative

Setting up a City of Sanctuary group

If there is not yet a City of Sanctuary initiative in your town or city, could you help to start one? This is not just for towns and cities with large refugee communities, or official 'dispersal areas'. Places with few refugees also play an important role in influencing the culture and public debate on sanctuary. The City of Sanctuary approach is also intended to be flexible enough to adapt to a specific local area, with its own history and character.

There many ways for towns or cities with very few refugees to build local support for people seeking sanctuary. These might include a 'twinning' arrangement with another city, to help with fundraising, or offering weekend breaks to refugee families. Many people seeking sanctuary in the UK are living in some of the most deprived areas of our large cities, and often have no opportunities to experience what the rest of the country is like.

For several years I helped to organise annual holidays to the seaside for a group of refugees from Liverpool. It was a wonderful experience to see children who are usually confined to a tiny inner-city flat able to play on the beach and swim in the sea. Their parents were also amazed that Britain could be so beautiful. One of the Iranian mothers told me wistfully that the coast of Abersoch in Wales was 'just like the Caspian Sea'.

Another exciting possibility is for a City of Sanctuary group to work on building local support in their town or city for hosting a refugee resettlement project through the United Nations Gateway Protection programme. This is a project that relocates very limited numbers of refugees from permanent camps in poor countries, to countries in the developed world which agree to take them. The Gateway programme also provides initial induction support, including resources for local schools to help with additional English provision for children. So far only a handful of British cities have accepted fairly small numbers of refugees through this programme, and City of Sanctuary groups could play a powerful role in encouraging their communities and local authorities to actively welcome a specific number of refugees in this way.

In areas which do have significant refugee communities there will probably be a range of existing refugee organisations and voluntary groups that provide practical support, legal advice, befriending and English tuition etc. Some of the people doing this work may question the need for a new refugee project, or be concerned about potential competition for funds and volunteers.

It is important to make it clear from the outset that City of Sanctuary is aiming to do something quite different to existing refugee organisations. Our aim is to encourage groups and organisations which don't have a specific focus on refugees to help with welcoming and including them. A successful City of Sanctuary initiative should be a means of widening the base of support for people seeking sanctuary, which in most areas is drawn from a small pool of highly committed people. Leicester City of Sanctuary, for example, has specifically focussed on broadening support for the local Red Cross destitution project by building up a network of new donors of food, clothing and money through their 'Golden Giver' scheme.

A local City of Sanctuary initiative might also work with existing refugee organisations to identify areas of need which are not currently being met. It could help to initiate the kind of practical responses that need broad-based support from the local community, such as voucher exchanges for people without access to cash support, or an emergency accommodation scheme.

Organisation structure

Most local City of Sanctuary groups have set up formal organisations, with a committee, constitution and bank account, and some have applied for charitable registration. This is not the only possible approach to creating a City of Sanctuary initiative though. Coventry City of Sanctuary has chosen to function as an informal network of organisations, with a 'task group' made up of representatives. They have found that this model saves on the administration involved in creating a new organisation with its own accounts and constitution. An unconstituted network like this can't apply for funds directly. Instead individual member organisations have raised funding to carry out City of Sanctuary-related activities.

Some City of Sanctuary working groups have also set up several sub-groups, doing specific tasks such as running events, or promoting the movement in particular 'sectors' such as education, local government, or business.

However a local City of Sanctuary initiative is structured, it is important to have a wide range of people involved, with contacts and expertise in different sectors and communities of their town or city. It is also important that a City of Sanctuary initiative is not led exclusively by refugee organisations. Refugee organisations will provide important expertise, contacts with refugee communities and in some cases practical help as well. (Refugee Action for example is supporting the movement by providing office space to local groups in Leicester and Bristol.) But a successful City of Sanctuary initiative needs to draw from a much wider base of support in the different communities and sectors of the city. For this purpose it is helpful to think strategically about the membership of a local City of Sanctuary working group, aiming to recruit people with contacts in universities, local business and the City Council etc. In Sheffield, having an influential Council member on our working group has proved vital in building a strong relationship with local government.

It is also helpful to find ways of building links with other local networks, such as faith forums, regeneration initiatives or 'Transition Town' movements. There is often scope for joint activities with networks like this, which can help to bring their membership into contact with people seeking sanctuary in your area.

Fundraising

A City of Sanctuary initiative doesn't have to rely on being able to raise large amounts of funding. It is possible to achieve a lot through the in-kind support of local organisations, and by asking for donations at public events. It will help, though, to have some funds available for volunteer expenses, printing, phone calls etc. There are usually small funds available locally to help with setting up community-based projects such as this, and it is worth asking for advice from local voluntary sector organisations such as Voluntary Action about how to apply for this money.

Local faith groups, Trades Unions, Student Unions and other groups can also make donations to good causes, usually with minimal form-filling involved. They are usually more likely to donate money to causes associated with someone they already know, so this is another reason to have working group members who are involved in many different organisations. Local supporters can also help raise money themselves. London's City of Sanctuary launch event was funded by volunteers running a sponsored half-marathon.

Larger sums for paid posts or more extensive projects may need to be raised from Charitable Trusts. Local groups will need to work together to co-ordinate their fundraising efforts when approaching national funders, and the national City of Sanctuary network can provide information and advice with this.

Pledges of support

A City of Sanctuary initiative aims to build a network of local organisations that actively welcome and include people seeking sanctuary in their activities.

To do this, we have developed 'pledges of support' that organisations can formally endorse in order to become official supporters (see Appendix for an example form). These pledge forms can be distributed at local events and individual volunteers can pass them on to their contacts in local organisations. We have found that it works best when organisations are contacted by people who are already 'insiders', who have existing relationships with the group being approached. These people can act as 'advocates' for the City of Sanctuary movement within the organisation. They will know the motivations and concerns of the people making the decision, and are less likely to be ignored than someone from outside approaching the organisation 'cold'.

When decision-makers are asked for a resolution of support, they have to discuss whether they want their organisation to include people seeking sanctuary or not. Having this conversation is a crucial first step in creating the possibility for cultural change. In many groups potentially controversial issues such as this tend to be avoided. By creating the need for this discussion, people have an opportunity to hear others' views and experiences about the situation of refugees. Whether or not they finally decide to pass the resolution of support, this is a useful process for helping people to examine their own attitudes and preconceptions.

Once an organisation passes a resolution of support for its local City of Sanctuary initiative, the next step is to try to translate this into some concrete actions or changes that will help people seeking sanctuary to be more fully included in its activities. One approach is to ask for details of a specific action commitment as part of the original pledge of support. Otherwise, the local City of Sanctuary group will need to follow up on initial pledges in order to encourage each organisation to find ways of putting it into practice.

This process can take time, especially with larger organisations, but we have found that it is worthwhile going through the formal procedures. As Bradford City of Sanctuary has reported:

"Whilst initially frustrated that some organisations took a very long time to sign up, and took the resolution through various committees first, we are learning that this is often better than knee-jerk signatures, as the campaign and its aims are properly made known and discussed. The Anglican Diocese was a case in point: we waited ages, hearing nothing, and then discovered that the Bishop had made it the subject of his Christmas message and written a 2 page insert to go in every church magazine in the Diocese!"

This is also a great opportunity for local groups to invite a refugee speaker who can share his or her own experiences of seeking sanctuary in your city. If there isn't already a group of refugees with experience of doing these kinds of talks, it would be a very useful project to organise training and support for them. I have been deeply impressed by the courage and enthusiasm of many refugees in Sheffield and other cities, who have been willing to share their experiences with local people in this way.

One of the main functions of a City of Sanctuary group is to help supporting organisations to think creatively about ways in which they can be more welcoming and inclusive to people seeking sanctuary in their community.

There are as many different ways of welcoming people seeking sanctuary as there are organisations. Supporting groups have offered free meeting space to refugee communities, provided volunteer placements and training courses, held fundraising events and publicised Refugee Week activities. Sheffield's community radio station has trained refugees to present their own regular shows, and a local magazine has offered a regular column for City of Sanctuary news. Some of the other ways that local organisations have found to include people seeking sanctuary are featured elsewhere in this book. Leicester City of Sanctuary has also held an event specifically to share ideas and good practice for how supporting organisations can be more inclusive and welcoming.

Some organisations may be limited in what they can offer practically, but symbolic support is also a contribution to influencing the local culture, especially if they can display a City of Sanctuary 'welcome' sign outside their premises.

By asking supporting organisations to pass on local City of Sanctuary news to their membership, you will also be building an extensive network for publicising events and activities, and appealing for volunteers or other needs of refugee communities.

It is a good idea from the beginning to create a database of the actions that supporting organisations are taking to implement their pledge of support. This will provide useful evidence of the impact of City of Sanctuary in your city for potential funders, media publicity and local government.

City of Sanctuary initiatives can also play a useful role in helping the organisers of local events and festivals to make links with refugee communities. Many groups such as festival organisers, museums, theatres, writing groups, libraries etc have an interest in finding new themes and reaching new audiences, but may need help with the right contacts in refugee communities, and support in developing ideas.

The Sheffield City of Sanctuary group has been a catalyst in this way for several joint projects, including a world music concert by Sheffield University Music department, a creative writing group sharing stories and experiences of different communities, and a museum display on Sheffield as a City of Sanctuary.

Rather than organising these projects ourselves, we aimed to bring the right people together to make them happen. It is a much more effective way to make refugees' participation part of the mainstream if an established institution such as a city museum or art gallery organises an exhibition rather than the City of Sanctuary group itself.

Statutory organisations

Although much of a City of Sanctuary initiative's early support is likely to come from voluntary and community groups, statutory organisations such as schools, hospitals, social services, the fire service, and police also provide important services for people seeking sanctuary and are also major employers in the city. It is important to try to involve these organisations in a City of Sanctuary initiative too.

Some City of Sanctuary groups have offered training to statutory organisations, to help them to understand the experience of people seeking sanctuary. This can also provide a source of funds for local groups, as most large organisations have training budgets they can use to pay for this service.

Coventry City of Sanctuary is also working with a local school to develop a model of a 'school of sanctuary'. The children themselves are working out criteria for what makes a school of sanctuary, and they aim to share this approach with other schools in the area.

Trades Unions can sometimes offer a way into opening communication even with unlikely organisations. Refugee speakers have been invited to speak to the UK Borders Agency reporting centre staff in Sheffield through their local union branch.

Working with the Council

The formal support of the City Council or other local authority is one of the criteria for becoming an official City of Sanctuary. The Council is a major employer and service provider for the city, and its policies and practices will have a significant effect on the lives of people seeking sanctuary.

There are legal restrictions on local Councils which mean that they cannot over-ride central government policy or decisions on individual asylum cases, but they do play a significant role in influencing local and national debate and political possibility. In some cases City Councils may also be willing to make formal resolutions in support of individuals, or call for changes in national government policy.

Many Councils are interested in the potential of grassroots initiatives for involving local people in decision-making. City of Sanctuary also offers a positive vision for the city, which can help to unite different communities, ('promoting social cohesion' in the jargon of the bureaucracy). Many Councillors are concerned about the situation of people seeking sanctuary. They may be frustrated at legal restrictions that prevent Councils from supporting those who are made destitute by refusal of their asylum claim. Supporting a local City of Sanctuary movement provides an opportunity for a constructive approach to these limitations. By working in partnership, the Council can make a significant contribution towards the shared goals of the movement, while other groups concentrate on the issues which the Council can't help with.

It is important that a Council resolution has cross-party support to prevent it becoming an issue for political wrangling, and to ensure continuity if the Council changes control. There may also be cities where it is very difficult to secure the support of the Council. In these cases it is still worth seeing Council endorsement as a long-term goal, even if this currently seems unlikely. Even without Council support, there is a great deal that local communities can do to create a more welcoming city for people seeking sanctuary. If this is successful, there is always potential for it to influence the wider political context of the city.

A local City of Sanctuary initiative will have to make a decision about the right time to approach their Council for a resolution of support. The process of building a grassroots local movement can be short-circuited by gaining Council endorsement too early. Council members are more likely to see their support as purely symbolic if there is not already a significant grassroots movement behind it. The worst case is that City of Sanctuary comes to be seen as a 'top-down' Council initiative, which will undermine personal ownership of the movement by local communities.

The ideal scenario is for a local City of Sanctuary initiative to build up sufficient grassroots support that the Council approaches them, wanting to offer their endorsement. This puts the local group in the useful situation of being able to make some specific requests about how Council support will be put into practice.

In practice, how this develops will depend on the local situation. In Sheffield, the City Council came to us with a resolution of support before we expected it, and probably before we were ready. At first this was largely a symbolic statement, without a commitment to any concrete actions.

Following this, we developed a Sheffield City of Sanctuary Manifesto, containing our long-terms goals for how the city welcomes and supports people seeking sanctuary (see www.cityofsanctuary.org/sheffield-manifesto). This Manifesto was later adopted by Sheffield City Council, making it official Council policy. We were then able to propose a series of recommendations for changes to Council policy and practice, in order to work towards these goals.

At the time of writing we are still in the process of working with the Council on the details of these action points, and have yet to see what the outcomes will be in practice. But it does offer a promising example of Council policy being developed from the bottom-up, through the suggestions and experience of a broad network of community organisations gathered through a local City of Sanctuary movement.

It is not necessarily the goal of a City of Sanctuary group to receive funding from the Council. This may be appropriate for some groups, but in this case they will need to find ways to ensure they retain their independence from Council control. The ideal is for the City of Sanctuary agenda to be embedded in the work of all Council departments. The City of Sanctuary initiative will need to agree a mechanism for regular liaison with the Council in order to make this happen. This might take the form of nominated Council officers responsible for promoting the City of Sanctuary's goals in the various departments. It is also helpful to get Councillors involved in advocating for the movement within the Council and in maintaining communication with the local group.

Some local campaigners may object to the idea of working with the Council in this way, especially where current Council practices are seen as harmful to people seeking sanctuary. There may be concern that a City Council could use the 'City of Sanctuary' label as political whitewash, to cover up the impact of their actual policies. In this case, some potential supporters may question whether they can encourage local people to take pride in the welcome they offer to refugees, when the reality falls far short of this ideal.

It is certainly crucial that the City of Sanctuary approach isn't hijacked by local government as a way of covering up its own shortcomings. This is why a city's 'official' status can only be conferred by the national City of Sanctuary movement, and not by the decision of a local Council. But in any town or city where there is a community of local people who are supporting people seeking sanctuary, this is already something to celebrate and a foundation for a City of Sanctuary initiative to build on.

Rather than accepting an inadequate Council's token endorsement, a local City of Sanctuary initiative can use the momentum of a growing popular movement to work for concrete changes in Council policy.

A City of Sanctuary initiative is a way of recognising the positive relationships that do already exist in a community, and emphasising their potential to improve life for everyone. This can be a much more powerful way of motivating people to get involved than just concentrating on the city's failings.

There is also a role for campaign groups which take a more confrontational approach towards local and national government, but it is more helpful to keep this separate from a City of Sanctuary movement. Our aim is to work on building the widespread local backing which will encourage Councils to work with us for positive change.

Campaigning

City of Sanctuary is not a political campaigning group, and we do not focus on trying to change national government policies directly. Instead, our aim is to contribute to cultural change through building local people's relationships with refugees in their community. This is based on the assumption that meaningful political change depends upon a shift in the public discussion about people seeking sanctuary in the UK.

Political campaigns are obviously important, and many of the people in a City of Sanctuary group will probably also be active in various campaign groups. The reason for keeping these activities separate is to enable the City of Sanctuary initiative to build the broadest possible coalition of support for the basic principle of offering sanctuary to people whose lives are in danger. There are many groups, including charities and others, which may be unwilling to endorse specific political campaigns, but which can unite around the broad principle of sanctuary. By demonstrating this public support, we aim to create a political context in which campaigns for changes in the asylum system will be more likely to succeed.

Similarly, City of Sanctuary groups do not organise anti-deportation campaigns on behalf of threatened individuals or families. This is a very important kind of action that local communities can take in defence of people whose claim for sanctuary has been refused, often as a result of inadequate legal help. We want to help build a culture in which local people stand up for their neighbours who are threatened, and who organise to defend them. But these campaigns have most credibility when they are built by local communities who have personal relationships with those threatened with deportation.

City of Sanctuary groups have helped to publicise local anti-deportation campaigns, and encourage supporters to find out more about the people affected, rather than organising these campaigns ourselves. There is already a national network of resources and support for individual anti-deportation campaigns in the National Coalition of Anti-Deportation Campaigns (www.ncadc.org.uk).

Peace Month, Coventry

Coventry City Council organises a peace month every year and invites organisations to put on a variety of events. In 2008, Coventry City of Sanctuary used this as an opportunity for local people to learn from newcomers to the city and organised four workshops to fit in with the overall programme we had devised:

1. **Personal – Inner Peace in Hard Circumstances.**
   Refugees escape extreme suffering in their home countries and often find further suffering such as imprisonment and destitution when they get here. Some of them share their experiences and how they cope.

2. **Peace in Relationships and Daily Life – Learning from Other Cultures**
   People from other countries share some of the things they do which aid harmony in relationships and daily life. An interactive event.

3. **Peace within and between Communities – is Coventry a City of Sanctuary?**
   How welcoming are we to newcomers to Coventry? With the help of a short film and discussions with forced and economic migrants we can learn about what we do well and gain ideas about what we could do better.

4. **International Peace – The Impact of the Arms Trade on African History**
   Centuries ago Britain sold guns to Africa in return for slaves and has continued to sell arms for political as well as financial gain ever since. We learn from Africans what impact this has.

All of these events gave refugees a voice and enabled local people to learn from their experiences. One of those attending commented that 'when N. told us about the way the police gave him chocolate when he arrived in this country I realised the huge impact that small acts of kindness can have."

It helped that the events all took place at the Peace House, which is a venue trusted by refugees and not too big. It is hard for people to share their distress when they spend so much of their time keeping it under control so they can cope with daily life. We asked people we knew and made sure they were well supported. On the walls were maps and an exhibition of art work by refugees.

We also did a day of campaigning in the city centre using street theatre, and again refugees themselves were the main activists. Everyone did what they felt comfortable with – handing out leaflets, talking to the public, acting in a tableau. We used the Friends Meeting House as a base where we could retreat from the public gaze for food and rest. We described ourselves as 'a roving band of performers and informers'. Everyone was very uplifted by the response we got. It was a risk and we had talked about dealing with hostility but in fact there was not a lot.

Peace Month enabled us to get a grant to pay for the Escape to Safety truck which is very effective in helping people understand why refugees flee, their journey here and their reception. It was in a school all week and other schools came to see it too. On the final day it was in the city centre. It was well worth the investment of money and time.

'But What Can We Do?' event, Leicester

In January 2009 a public meeting was organised by Leicester City of Sanctuary for individuals and organisations to find out what they can do to help people seeking sanctuary in Leicester.

Speakers included the British Red Cross and Refugee Action, who talked about volunteer involvement in their projects and services. A local church group also spoke about what they had done since hearing an appeal for support for destitute asylum seekers four months ago. They have made regular donations of food to the British Red Cross, hosted a Christmas event and given the 100+ guests a food hamper each to take away, and organised a coach, food and volunteers for an amazing day out at the seaside.

Sessions were held in the afternoon and evening to enable the maximum number of people to attend, with an overall turnout of over 60. Following the presentations participants split into groups to discuss ways they could support people seeking sanctuary, and/or the organisations that are working with them. Suggestions which came out of those discussions and which volunteers took forward include:

- additional drop-off points for food donations for the British Red Cross.

- 'Meet and Greet' in Rupert Street - volunteers to meet, greet and provide refreshments and toast to those waiting at Refugee Action drop-ins.

- a monthly news digest of news and other information, available from various sources but not previously well circulated.

The ideas generated will be compiled into a hand-out for use at events. They will also be used when giving presentations to groups, as examples of ways to get involved in supporting people seeking sanctuary in our community.

Lord Mayor's Reception for People Seeking Sanctuary, Oxford

In March 2009, the Lord Mayor of Oxford, Susanna Pressel, held a reception for people seeking sanctuary in the city, as part of the Council's commitment to support Oxford becoming a City of Sanctuary.

The event was attended by about 20 people seeking sanctuary in Oxford, as well as representatives from local refugee organisations Refugee Resource, Asylum Welcome and Open Door, and journalists from BBC Radio Oxford and the Oxford Mail.

Susanna Pressel thanked those attending for the contributions that they have made to Oxford and spoke about the contributions that refugees have made to the City over the years, as well as talking about her own refugee roots. She also asked the guests to tell her and the Council what needs to be done to better assist refugees.

The event attracted some positive media coverage. Amy Merone from the City of Sanctuary group in Oxford did a live interview with BBC Radio Oxford on the afternoon of the reception. She spoke about the poistive contribution that people seeking sanctuary and refugees have made and continue to make in Oxford, while also highlighting the need for better support for people going through the asylum process and a better understanding of the issues from the general public.

One man who is a refugee from Zimbabwe was interviewed for BBC Radio Oxford and his story was then featured for three consecutive mornings on the Breakfast Show. The journalist who conducted this interview has since asked to meet to talk about developing similar story ideas. There was also a piece in the Oxford Mail, featuring quotes from people seeking sanctuary, highlighting both the contributions that they have made to Oxford and also the challenges that they face here.

SIX

Becoming an official City of Sanctuary

The National City of Sanctuary Network

The national City of Sanctuary movement is organised as a network of independent local groups, with a shared set of core principles (see Appendix). We hold regular national network meetings for representatives of local groups to meet and exchange ideas and experience. Decisions affecting the whole movement, such as the statement of core principles, are taken at these meetings using a consensus approach.

Local groups have found this network a useful way of learning from each others' experience. It also provides a way for groups to co-ordinate national initiatives and publicity, such as a national tour of the Actors for Human Rights play 'Asylum Dialogues' for Refugee Week 2009.

There is also a national City of Sanctuary charity, which employs the National Co-ordinator and has responsibility for promoting and supporting new City of Sanctuary initiatives throughout the UK.

The City of Sanctuary National Co-ordinator is employed on a part-time basis, funded by the Joseph Rowntree Charitable Trust, to provide support to local City of Sanctuary initiatives, and to develop the national network. This includes being available to speak at local launch events, developing promotional literature and resources, and offering information and advice on the practicalities of setting up a City of Sanctuary initiative, as well as writing this handbook.

The national City of Sanctuary website (at www.cityofsanctuary. org) is another important resource for local groups. It has a facility for each local group to have its own section for their news, publicity, photos, video or audio recordings, documents etc.

Local City of Sanctuary groups can manage their own website content directly, using simple web-forms to input articles and attach pictures and documents.

Making good use of the website is a very effective way to recruit and communicate with supporters, as long as it is kept up to date and well-stocked with interesting content. As your initiative will hopefully grow rapidly, and printed information quickly becomes out of date, it is also much cheaper to produce publicity which directs the public to your web address for the latest news.

There is also a 'blog' section on the website (at www.city ofsanctuary.org/blog) for publishing personal stories, experiences, poetry, photos or video by anyone involved in the City of Sanctuary movement, whether people seeking sanctuary themselves or their friends and supporters. This is a very flexible and effective medium for communicating directly with the public about your experiences and the issues which seldom receive fair treatment in the mainstream media.

Several City of Sanctuary initiatives have also set up group webpages on social networking sites such as Facebook. This is a quick and easy way of attracting new potential supporters, who can automatically invite their friends to join the group. A majority of users of these sites tend to be younger people, so this is also a good way of reaching them. It is then easy to send publicity about events or requests for support to all members of the Facebook group at once.

Criteria for becoming a City of Sanctuary

In order to have a consistent message about what it means to be a City of Sanctuary, it is essential to have a set of criteria for deciding when a town or city has achieved 'official' City of Sanctuary status.

Our current criteria have been developed by the national City of Sanctuary network and approved by the representatives of local groups. They are intended to be clear enough to offer a coherent identity for the City of Sanctuary movement, but also to provide for the flexibility to fit these aims to the local situation in the most relevant way.

There are four key criteria to becoming a 'City of Sanctuary'. To be recognised as an official Town or City of Sanctuary, the local City of Sanctuary working group will need to achieve these four essential goals:

1. Resolutions of support from a significant and representative proportion of local groups and organisations. These should include a commitment from supporting organisations to welcome and include people seeking sanctuary in the groups' activities, and evidence of practical efforts to build relationships between those seeking sanctuary and local people.

2. The support and involvement of local refugee communities, and refugee representation on the local City of Sanctuary working group.

3. A resolution of support from the City Council (or other Local Authority). This will include a specific commitment to becoming a welcoming city for refugees and people seeking sanctuary, as well as co-operation with the local City of Sanctuary movement in policy and strategy making.

4. A strategy, agreed by the main supporting organisations, for how the city is to continue working towards greater inclusion of refugees and people seeking sanctuary. Continued progress will be measured by an annual review process.

It is important to recognise that a resolution of support from the Local Authority is only one of the criteria for becoming a City of Sanctuary. This is because without real community involvement support from the local Council could easily be a purely token resolution, with little practical impact on the experience of people seeking sanctuary. Although obtaining the support of the Council is necessary to obtain City of Sanctuary status, it is the participation of local community organisations which has priority.

We have not set precise targets for how many supporting organisations are needed, as this will vary hugely with the size of city. It is up to the local City of Sanctuary group to estimate what 'a significant and representative proportion' of local organisations means for their town or city.

In addition, the town or city should be able to demonstrate public awareness and involvement in support for people seeking sanctuary, through meeting a range of goals from the following list (or similar):

- Workshops for schools on sanctuary issues.
- Social and cultural events where people seeking sanctuary and local people interact.
- Speakers' events for local people to hear from those seeking sanctuary directly about their experiences.
- Concerts and drama productions by refugee artists.
- Signs displayed by supporting organisations to welcome people seeking sanctuary.
- Interfaith events promoting sanctuary and hospitality.
- Community conflict resolution services for areas experiencing tension over new arrivals.
- Work with local media to publicise positive stories of people seeking sanctuary.
- Involvement of refugees in media production.
- Civic receptions for new arrivals in the city.
- Refugee community involvement in festivals and cultural events.
- Programme of events and activities for Refugee Week.
- Programmes for employment training and voluntary work placements for refugees and those seeking sanctuary.

These activities will not necessarily be organised by the City of Sanctuary group itself. In many areas there will be other organisations which already undertake this kind of work. What is important is that this kind of activity should be present in the town or city, as evidence of the practical engagement of local people in support for people seeking sanctuary.

Process for recognition of a City of Sanctuary

At the time of writing, only Sheffield has announced 'official' City of Sanctuary status, although several other groups are well on their way to meeting these criteria. The process that we have agreed for official recognition as a Town or City of Sanctuary is therefore largely untried so far, and may be developed or adapted as we gain more experience of using it.

The central feature of the process is that it is the national network which acts as the 'accrediting body' for becoming an official City of Sanctuary. A City Council or other local authority cannot confer this status itself.

The key steps of the process that we have identified are roughly in this order.

1. The local working group develops its own goals and strategy for meeting the City of Sanctuary criteria outlined above, in a way that is relevant to their situation. The group maintains regular contact with the national network in order to share reports on progress, ideas and resources.

2. When the local group has achieved its initial goals, it reports to the national network group (composed of all City of Sanctuary working groups) and proposes making an official announcement of 'City of Sanctuary' status.

3. The national group may ask questions, make suggestions, or recommend further work that may need to be done.

4. When there is agreement by the national network group that the criteria have been met, the local group can announce its achievement of 'official' City of Sanctuary status, which will be recognised and publicised by the national movement.

5. Following recognition as an official City of Sanctuary, the local group will continue to support the development of a culture of hospitality and to monitor continued progress towards its long term goals.

Becoming an official Town or City of Sanctuary is a significant achievement, recognising a widespread and influential local movement of support for people seeking sanctuary. It does not mean, though, that there is no more to be done. Inevitably, the process of including people seeking sanctuary in the community is a continuing task, and there will be many barriers to their full participation which still need to be overcome. This is why it is necessary for an official City of Sanctuary to have a strategy for how to continue promoting the participation of people seeking sanctuary in the future.

This doesn't necessarily mean that the City of Sanctuary group will have to continue indefinitely. Ideally, the goal of extending hospitality towards people seeking sanctuary should be adopted fully by all of the organisations in the city, so that a City of Sanctuary working group is no longer needed.

In practice though, this is likely to be a long-term objective, and the City of Sanctuary group will need to maintain its work in some form, in order to keep the movement growing and developing.

It is still early days for the national City of Sanctuary movement. Groups all over the country have already shown a wonderful creativity and enthusiasm in developing the movement's potential in new directions. It has been a constant source of inspiration and encouragement for me to visit city after city, everywhere meeting communities of people working together to build a more welcoming and hospitable society. I would like to thank all of them for their contribution to building this movement, and invite you to take part in making your town or city a place of sanctuary.

If you would like to get involved in your local City of Sanctuary initiative, you can get in touch with them through the website at: www.cityofsanctuary.org

If there is not yet a City of Sanctuary group in your area, and you could help to start one, please let us know. You can contact me at: craig@cityofsanctuary.org

APPENDIX

City of Sanctuary Core Principles

1. City of Sanctuary is a mainstream, grassroots movement.

Local groups work to build coalitions of organisations from all sectors (faith groups, voluntary, business, education, etc) which make a public commitment to welcome and include refugees and people seeking sanctuary in their usual activities. Local working groups should be representative of different sectors, not just refugee organisations, and the endorsement of local government should be sought on the basis of demonstrated community support, rather than being a 'top-down' council initiative.

2. City of Sanctuary works by creating opportunities for relationships between local people and those seeking sanctuary.

Where local organisations and communities include people seeking sanctuary in their activities, personal relationships will be formed which will lead to greater understanding and support from the host community. City of Sanctuary seeks to influence the political debate on sanctuary indirectly through cultural change, and does not engage in political lobbying or anti-deportation campaigns directly.

3. City of Sanctuary offers a positive vision of a culture of hospitality for those in need of safety.

We encourage communities to take pride in offering a place of safety for people whose lives are threatened, and celebrating their contribution to our towns and cities. The focus is on those people who are forced to seek sanctuary rather than voluntary migration or diversity in general. At the same time we intend that the process of working for a culture of hospitality will also benefit other migrant groups, as well as host communities.

Action ideas

Some of the activities that City of Sanctuary groups have planned or carried out so far include:

- Workshops for schools on sanctuary issues.

- Ceilidh dances, 'Life Swaps', and other social events where people seeking sanctuary and local people can meet and interact.

- Speakers' events for local people to hear from those seeking sanctuary directly about their experiences.

- Concerts and drama productions by refugee artists.

- Producing signs for display by supporting organisations to welcome people seeking sanctuary.

- Interfaith events promoting sanctuary and hospitality.

- Community conflict resolution training for areas experiencing tension over new arrivals.

- Work with local media to publicise positive stories of people seeking sanctuary.

- Involvement of people seeking sanctuary in media production.

- Civic receptions for new arrivals in the city.

- Refugee community involvement in festivals and cultural events.

- Voluntary work placements for refugees and those seeking sanctuary.

- Public signing of resolutions of support by local organisation representatives.

- Inclusion of City of Sanctuary goals in Local Strategic Partnership strategies.

CITY OF SANCTUARY

RESOLUTION OF SUPPORT

....*(name of organisation)* recognises the contribution of asylum-seekers and refugees to the City of Sheffield, and is committed to welcoming and including them in our activities. We support Sheffield being a recognised 'City of Sanctuary' for refugees and asylum-seekers.

The specific action which our organisation will take to make our activities more inclusive for people seeking sanctuary is

....

....

(See www.cityofsanctuary.org/suggestions for some ideas)

Signed ....

Position within organisation (This should be a committee member or equivalent)

....

Date .... Email ....

Organisation address ....

....

Please sign and return to:
City of Sanctuary, Victoria Hall, Norfolk Street, Sheffield S1 2JB

City of Sanctuary is a national movement to build a culture of hospitality for people seeking sanctuary in the UK. Its goal is to create a network of towns and cities throughout the UK which are proud to be places of safety, and which include people seeking sanctuary fully in the life of their communities.

www.cityofsanctuary.org/sheffield

<u>Notes</u>

Notes

Notes

Notes

Notes

Notes

<u>Notes</u>

Notes

<u>Notes</u>

Notes

Notes